SCIEN

AND INVENTORS

written by Danny Clarke
illustrated by John Dillow

CONTENTS

WHAT ARE SCIENTISTS AND INVENTORS?

Scientists are people who try to find out why certain things happen or how things are made. They come up with **theories** to explain things, and test these theories by doing experiments. An inventor is anyone who thinks of new machines or new ways of making things.

Who are they?

Anyone can be a scientist or an inventor. Perhaps one day you may think up an important scientific theory or create your own invention.

EARLY INVENTORS

The very first inventors made hand tools to help them cut up food and carve wood. Early people made very important discoveries such as how to make fire and how to work with metal, and invented the wheel and the plough. These developments changed the way people lived and led to many other discoveries and inventions.

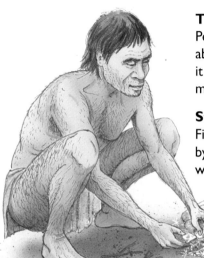

The discovery of fire
People discovered how to make fire about 500,000 years ago. They used it for light, heat and cooking, and to make tools and weapons from metal.

Starting a fire
Fires were often started by rubbing two bits of wood, or flint, together.

The invention of the wheel
The wheel was first used about 5,500 years ago in Mesopotamia, a region of southwest Asia. The first wheels were made in three wooden sections that were joined together. Spoked wheels were invented later, in Roman times.

Roman spoked wheel

Early wheel

The plough

Ploughs were first used about 6,000 years ago to turn soil and break it up. Using ploughs meant that the land could be farmed by fewer people so others were free to do different tasks.

Metalworking

Most metals are found in rocks called ores. They are usually combined with other substances, such as oxygen. Heat is needed to obtain the metals from their ores. This process is called smelting. Copper ore and iron ore were the first metals to be smelted.

Copper ore

Iron ore

THE GREEK CIVILISATION

The ancient Greeks were some of the first people to think about how the world works. People called **philosophers** came up with theories to explain the things they saw around them. The Greeks were very good at mathematics and **astronomy**, and they also invented many useful machines such as the Archimedes' screw.

Plato and Aristotle
Plato and Aristotle were two famous Greek philosophers who theorised about the world around them. The word 'Philosophy' comes from a Greek word meaning 'love of wisdom'.

Archimedes

The Greek mathematician, Archimedes, is most famous for his cry of 'Eureka!' which he shouted when he stepped in the bath and discovered why things float. He also invented the Archimedes' screw, which was used for lifting water and grain.

Eureka!

'Eureka', is a Greek word, meaning 'I have found it'.

Archimedes' screw

By turning the handle at one end of the screw, water is lifted up the tube and onto the land.

Measuring the Earth

Eratosthenes was an early Greek astronomer and mathematician. He was also in charge of a huge library in the Greek city of Alexandria. Eratosthenes believed that the Earth was round, like a ball. He worked out the Earth's size by measuring the length of a shadow at noon on midsummer's day. Amazingly, his answer was very close to the actual size of the Earth, as measured using the **technology** of today.

THE ALCHEMISTS

In ancient Greece, India and China, many people believed that the world was based on opposites, such as hot and cold, or male and female. They believed that gold was a pure, or 'good' metal, while lead was an impure, or 'bad' metal. The alchemists were people who experimented with metals to see if they could change lead into gold.

Alchemists' laboratories
The alchemists did experiments on many different substances in well-equipped laboratories. They heated substances over fires and carefully wrote down what happened during their experiments.

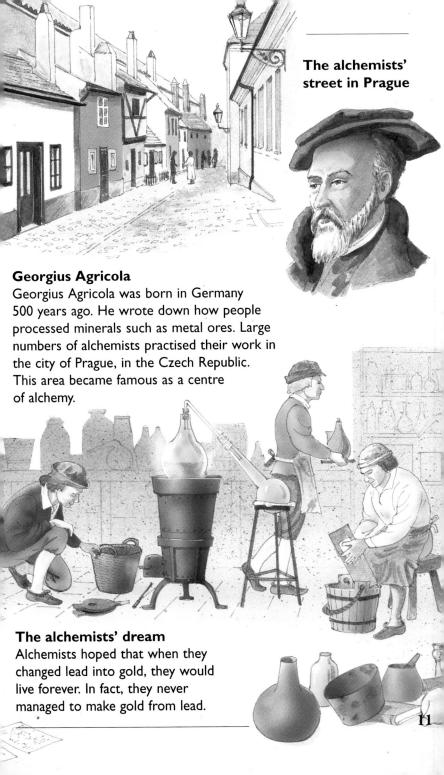

The alchemists' street in Prague

Georgius Agricola

Georgius Agricola was born in Germany 500 years ago. He wrote down how people processed minerals such as metal ores. Large numbers of alchemists practised their work in the city of Prague, in the Czech Republic. This area became famous as a centre of alchemy.

The alchemists' dream

Alchemists hoped that when they changed lead into gold, they would live forever. In fact, they never managed to make gold from lead.

11

LAWS OF THE UNIVERSE

From early times, people believed that the Earth was at the centre of the Universe. In 1543 a Polish astronomer, Nicolaus Copernicus, put forward the theory that the Sun was at the centre of our Solar System. Later, Galileo Galilei in Italy and Isaac Newton in England confirmed this theory through **observation** and calculation.

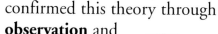

Nicolaus Copernicus

GALILEO AND THE TELESCOPE

Galileo was one of the first people to look at the Moon and planets using a telescope. He made very careful observations which led to many discoveries. The most important one was that the Earth moves round the Sun.

Galileo in trouble

Galileo was put on trial and imprisoned by the Roman Catholic Church. This was because many of his discoveries went against the beliefs of the Church at the time, who thought that the Sun went round the Earth.

Isaac Newton

The English scientist Isaac Newton was born in 1642, the year Galileo died. Newton made very important discoveries about forces and motion, about light and colour and about mathematics. He realised that **gravity**, which made an apple fall from a tree, held the Moon in orbit round the Earth, and the Earth round the Sun.

DISCOVERING MATTER

People have always asked what **matter** is actually made of. The first person to experiment carefully enough to begin discovering the answer was French **chemist** Antoine Lavoisier. He lived at a time when scientists found new theories to explain matter and electricity – their experiments proved some of the theories correct.

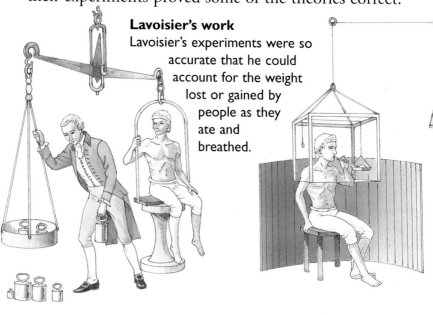

Lavoisier's work
Lavoisier's experiments were so accurate that he could account for the weight lost or gained by people as they ate and breathed.

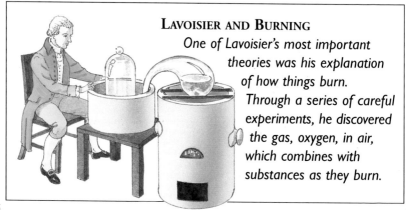

LAVOISIER AND BURNING
One of Lavoisier's most important theories was his explanation of how things burn. Through a series of careful experiments, he discovered the gas, oxygen, in air, which combines with substances as they burn.

Volta and the electric battery

Italian scientist Alessandro Volta was the first person to make a battery. It was made from copper and zinc discs, separated by paper discs soaked in acid.

Layers

A section from Volta's battery, showing the different layers.

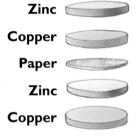

Zinc
Copper
Paper
Zinc
Copper

Volta with his battery

Electromagnetism

In 1821, a Danish scientist called Hans Oersted discovered that an electric current always produces **magnetism**. English **physicist** Michael Faraday investigated this effect and made many more discoveries about electricity and magnetism. His inventions include an electric motor and a generator.

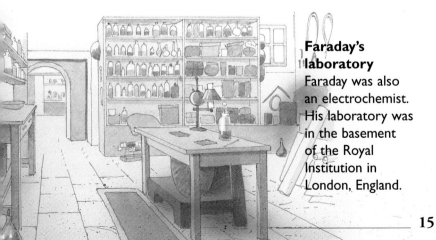

Faraday's laboratory
Faraday was also an electrochemist. His laboratory was in the basement of the Royal Institution in London, England.

EVOLUTION

An important theory in science is the theory of **evolution**. It explains how so many different types, or **species**, of plant and animal came into existence. English **biologist** Charles Darwin came up with this theory after studying thousands of different plants and animals. He realised how different species are related to each other.

TECHNOLOGY AND THE CAR

Around 500 years ago, in the time of Leonardo da Vinci, there were no cars. People could only move around on land by foot, on horseback or in a horse-drawn cart. Da Vinci dreamed of a car that could move under its own power, but the first car was built more than 350 years after his death.

The first kind of car, powered by a steam engine, was built by French engineer Nicholas Cugnot in 1770. Nowadays, cars are designed to be as safe as possible. This is due to inventions such as airbags, seat belts, side impact bars and anti-lock braking systems. Computers are also used in modern cars to control the engine.

The engine

In 1878 a German, Nikolaus August Otto, built a gas-powered combustion engine. By 1884 Gottlieb Daimler became the first person to make a high-speed, light-weight petrol engine. Karl Benz made a three-wheeled vehicle powered by a petrol **internal combustion engine** in 1885 which had a maximum speed of 13 kilometres per hour. Rudolph Diesel first built a diesel engine in 1892. Another type of internal combustion engine was invented in 1956 by the German engineer Karl Wankel.

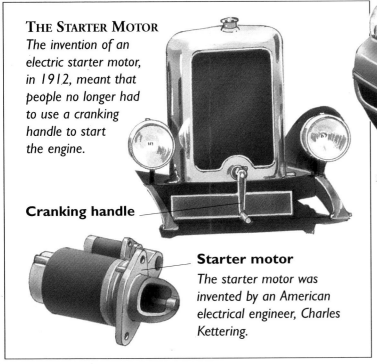

THE STARTER MOTOR
The invention of an electric starter motor, in 1912, meant that people no longer had to use a cranking handle to start the engine.

Cranking handle

Starter motor
The starter motor was invented by an American electrical engineer, Charles Kettering.

Tyres

The pneumatic (filled with air) tyre was originally patented by Robert Thomson in 1845. John Boyd Dunlop first began to use pneumatic tyres in 1887 when he fitted them to his bicycle. The first successful pneumatic tyres for cars were made in 1895 by French brothers, André and Edouard Michelin.

Galapagos Islands

Darwin took careful notes while on the Galapagos Islands off South America. The notes supported his theory of evolution, which explains how species that are well suited to their surroundings will survive, while others will become extinct, or die off. This idea is called natural selection.

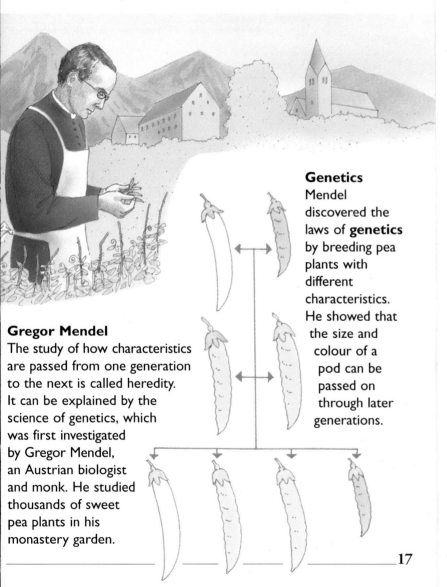

Gregor Mendel

The study of how characteristics are passed from one generation to the next is called heredity. It can be explained by the science of genetics, which was first investigated by Gregor Mendel, an Austrian biologist and monk. He studied thousands of sweet pea plants in his monastery garden.

Genetics

Mendel discovered the laws of **genetics** by breeding pea plants with different characteristics. He showed that the size and colour of a pod can be passed on through later generations.

LEONARDO DA VINCI

Leonardo da Vinci was one of the greatest inventors of all time. He was born in Vinci, near Florence in Italy, in 1452. He was a great scientist and inventor, and also a great artist. He created one of the most famous paintings of all time – the Mona Lisa.

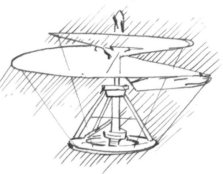

Leonardo da Vinci

Helicopter

The first helicopters were built in the 20th century. Leonardo thought up this idea for a helicopter 400 years earlier.

Ahead of his time

Many of da Vinci's ideas could not have worked in his lifetime, because there were no ways to make the materials needed or to provide the necessary power.

Windscreen wipers

Mechanical windscreen wipers were first used in America in 1916.

The Model T

In 1908 Henry Ford introduced a successful method of producing lots of cars quickly and economically. They were manufactured on an assembly line which made them cheaper. Fifteen million Model Ts were sold in many countries of the world. Model Ts were able to travel at a speed of up to 64 kilometres per hour.

The Mini

The Mini was first introduced in 1959. It was designed by Alec Issigonis and built by the Austin company. The Mini has since become very popular and has been used for many different purposes – from police car to rally car.

Catalytic converters

The exhaust fumes from car engines contain many gases which pollute the air. As more and more cars use our roads, the levels of air pollution increase. In 1979 the catalytic converter was invented. This is a device which is fitted between the engine and the exhaust outflow to reduce some types of pollution. New cars must be fitted with catalytic converters.

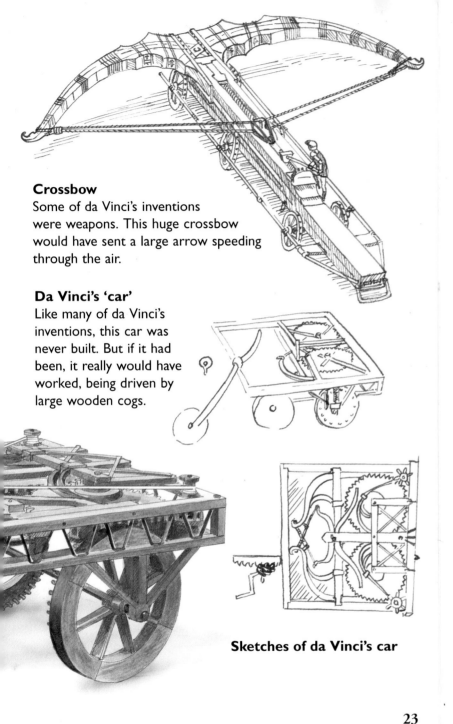

Crossbow
Some of da Vinci's inventions were weapons. This huge crossbow would have sent a large arrow speeding through the air.

Da Vinci's 'car'
Like many of da Vinci's inventions, this car was never built. But if it had been, it really would have worked, being driven by large wooden cogs.

Sketches of da Vinci's car

THE DOUBLE HELIX

The theory of evolution explained how new types of plants and animals come to exist. Genetics showed how different characteristics were passed from generation to generation, but scientists wanted to find out how this worked. They discovered that a chemical called DNA (deoxyribonucleic acid) was responsible.

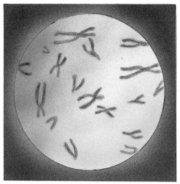

Under the microscope
In 1882, tiny parts of cells called chromosomes were first observed under a microscope. Chromosomes contain DNA.

X-ray crystallography
A technique called X-ray crystallography was used to discover the structure of DNA. This technique was developed by father and son, William Lawrence Bragg and William Henry Bragg.

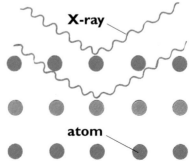

X-ray

atom

Discovering the structure
In X-ray crystallography high-power X-rays reflect off the atoms in a substance. The positions of atoms in the substance can be worked out from how the X-rays are reflected.

Francis Crick

DNA model

Rosalind Franklin

DNA molecule

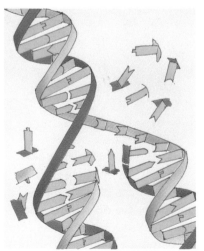

James Watson

The double helix

DNA is present in all plant and animal cells. It is vital in passing on personal characteristics and making each of us individual. Rosalind Franklin studied the structure of DNA using X-ray crystallography. In 1953 James Watson and Francis Crick used her work to construct a model of DNA, which they found to have a double helix shape.

MEDICAL BREAKTHROUGHS

Doctors have always been concerned with preventing and curing diseases. Modern doctors understand that germs are the root cause of many familiar diseases. But the connection between germs and diseases was not made until the 1850s. Diseases can be cured by using drugs, called antibiotics, and can be prevented by using chemicals, called antiseptics, and by vaccination.

Vaccination

Edward Jenner was the first person to perform a vaccination. He noticed that milkmaids never caught a disease called smallpox, although they did catch a similar disease called cowpox. Jenner had a theory that the cowpox was protecting the milkmaids from smallpox. He deliberately infected a healthy boy with cowpox – the boy never caught smallpox. It is now known that the cowpox made the boy's body produce chemicals called antibodies that protected him from smallpox.

Success

Following his successful vaccination of the boy, Jenner went on to treat many more people.

Antiseptics

French chemist Louis Pasteur found tiny living things called micro-organisms, or germs, living in milk which turned it bad. This observation led to a theory to explain why many people became infected by germs when they had a cut or an operation.

English surgeon, Joseph Lister, used carbolic acid in operations which saved many people's lives.

Carbolic acid

Carbolic acid is an antiseptic which kills germs and prevents infection by disease.

RELATIVITY, LIGHT AND SOUND

German-born physicist Albert Einstein was a truly brilliant scientist, most famous for his theories of relativity. He published the theory of special relativity in 1905 and general relativity in 1916. Einstein's theories of relativity gave scientists a new way of looking at time and space, and a new way of understanding gravity.

Time slows down

Special relativity states that time runs slower at high speeds. This idea was proved correct in an experiment on a plane at Chesapeake Bay, America. The plane flew round the world – returning earlier than predicted.

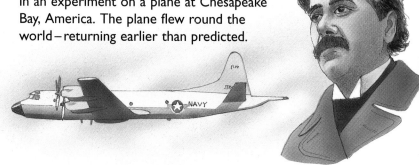

Space and gravity

General relativity explains gravity by showing that space around an object is 'curved', just as a stretched sheet of rubber is when an object is placed on it.

Thought experiments

Einstein's theories were based on so-called 'thought' experiments. These were done in his head or using mathematics. Later, real experiments proved him correct.

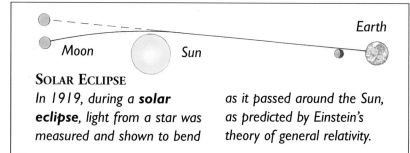

SOLAR ECLIPSE
*In 1919, during a **solar eclipse**, light from a star was measured and shown to bend as it passed around the Sun, as predicted by Einstein's theory of general relativity.*

Thomas Edison

American inventor, Thomas Edison, was involved in many of the important inventions of the past 100 years. He took out over 1,000 patents – documents that a person writes to claim an invention as his or her original idea. It means that no one else can use these ideas without the permission of the inventor.

Electric light

The electric light bulb was invented by two people quite separately. Edison was one, and Joseph Swan, in England, was the other.

Sound recording

Edison was the first to record and play back sound, using his invention, the 'phonograph' (below). The name phonograph, means 'sound writing'.

Research laboratory

Edison set up a well-equipped laboratory where he and his employees worked on new inventions.

TRAVEL AND COMMUNICATION

The world has changed dramatically over the last 200 years. Many of the things we do today, such as talk on the telephone, watch television or travel in a plane, have been made possible by the work of many scientists and inventors.

Photography

The invention of photography provided an important way of communicating using pictures. The first cameras, made during the 1830s, were developed from the 'camera obscura', a device that helped artists to make accurate drawings.

Camera obscura

An inverted image of the person is projected on to the rear wall of a dark box.

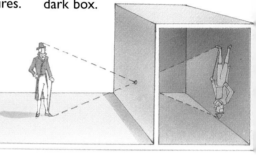

The telephone

Before the invention of the telephone, the fastest way to communicate with people who were far away was by using the telegraph. This involved sending pulses of electricity along wires, in Morse code. With the telephone we can speak to people who are hundreds or thousands of kilometres away.

Whose invention?

Alexander Graham Bell and Elisha Gray both applied for patents for the telephone on the same day in February 1876, but Bell was awarded the patent.

The Lumière brothers

Many people were involved in the invention of moving pictures – the cinema. The Lumière brothers put on the first public showing of a film in 1895. The film showed people leaving a factory. The audiences were amazed at the sight of moving images on the screen.

The television

Like cinema, television was invented through the collective work of many people. Television pictures were first transmitted in 1926, by Scottish inventor, John Logie Baird.

The Rocket

The railways

The invention of the steam train in the 1830s made travel easier and quicker. Before this, people rode horses or travelled in horse-drawn carriages. 'The Rocket' was one of the first trains to transport people.

The motor car

The invention of the internal combustion engine made cars a real possibility. German engineer Karl Benz was the first person to sell a car, in 1885.

The helicopter

German, Heinrich Focke, built the first helicopter in 1936.

RADIOACTIVITY AND THE ATOM

The idea that matter is made of tiny particles called atoms was first thought of in ancient Greece. By the 1800s, there was widespread belief in the existence of atoms. Until 1897, they were thought of as the smallest particles of matter, but the discovery of the **electron**, and **radioactivity** from the atom's nucleus proved otherwise.

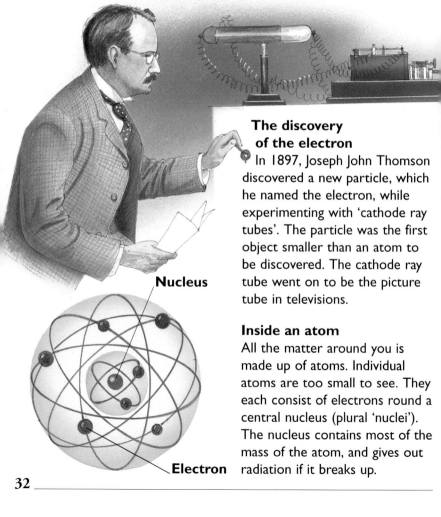

Nucleus

Electron

The discovery of the electron

In 1897, Joseph John Thomson discovered a new particle, which he named the electron, while experimenting with 'cathode ray tubes'. The particle was the first object smaller than an atom to be discovered. The cathode ray tube went on to be the picture tube in televisions.

Inside an atom

All the matter around you is made up of atoms. Individual atoms are too small to see. They each consist of electrons round a central nucleus (plural 'nuclei'). The nucleus contains most of the mass of the atom, and gives out radiation if it breaks up.

Marie Curie

Atoms become radioactive when their nuclei break up. The radiation they give out can be harmful. French physicist Marie Curie investigated radioactivity and discovered much about the atom. However, Curie's research gave her cancer, from which she eventually died.

John Cockcroft ⊥ Ernest Walton

Splitting the atom

An atom's nucleus is made of two particles – protons and neutrons. Cockcroft and Walton fired protons at nuclei, and saw the nuclei change – in many cases split in half, each forming two smaller nuclei.

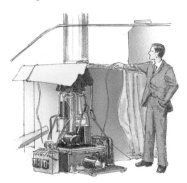

Science and society

Walton and Cockcroft's discovery led to the manufacture of the atom bomb during the Second World War. It is an example of a destructive discovery which has created a source of concern.

33

SCIENTISTS AND INVENTORS TODAY

Modern scientists investigate all kinds of specialised subjects. The computer has become an essential tool for nearly all scientists. Most inventors today also need to understand the theories of science, as most inventions are quite complicated. However, some of the best inventions are also the most simple.

Working with computers
Most scientists use computers to help their research. They use computers to analyse and display information collected from experiments. Many inventors use computers to help them design their inventions, too.

PICTURES OF THE UNIVERSE
For a long time scientists have been interested in finding out how the universe began. Special telescopes probe far into space and send back data to powerful computers which produce pictures like this one. The pictures can help to prove or disprove theories about the universe.

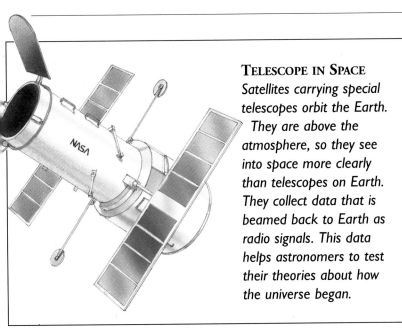

TELESCOPE IN SPACE

Satellites carrying special telescopes orbit the Earth. They are above the atmosphere, so they see into space more clearly than telescopes on Earth. They collect data that is beamed back to Earth as radio signals. This data helps astronomers to test their theories about how the universe began.

DNA fingerprints

Using discoveries

DNA is a chemical that is present in all living things. Everyone's DNA is different, and by analysing a person's DNA structure, an individual can be identified. This process, called DNA fingerprinting, is being used successfully by the police force. This is a good example of how modern scientific inventions contribute to society.

35

AMAZING SCIENTISTS & INVENTORS FACTS

- **The meaning of 'atom'** The word atom comes from the Greek word 'atomein', which means 'something which you cannot divide'.

- **Strange theories** Until about 200 years ago heat, electricity, light and magnetism were thought to be fluids (like water) that passed between objects. They are now all known to be different types of energy.

- **Accidental discoveries** Many important discoveries are made by accident. For example, penicillin is an antibiotic (a type of medicine) that was accidentally discovered by Alexander Fleming in 1928. Fleming noticed that some germs had been killed in one of his experiments by some mould that had landed in a dish in his laboratory!

- **Scientific journals** It is important that scientists communicate their ideas to each other. They often do this by writing the results of their experiments in scientific journals. In 1750, there were only about ten journals printed regularly. In 1830 there were 300, and today there are about 40,000.

- **Valuable discovery** By taking out a patent, inventors achieve two things. They prove that their invention was their own idea, and they are in a position to claim money if the invention is sold. The patent for the telephone, which was given to Alexander Graham Bell, was probably the most valuable one in history.

- **Grand unified theory** Some scientists today are trying to find one theory to explain everything in the universe. Such a theory is called a grand unified theory.

GLOSSARY

Astronomy The study of the universe and its stars, planets and comets.

Biologist A scientist involved in this study of living things.

Chemist A person involved in the study of how substances react together.

Electron A tiny particle found in every atom. Moving electrons make up the flow of electric current in a wire.

Evolution The process by which plant and animal species develop over time.

Genetics A branch of biology which deals with how characteristics are passed from generation to generation.

Gravity A force that pulls objects together. Gravity pulls you and the Earth together, and this gives you weight.

Internal combustion engine The type of engine which burns fuel inside cylinders.

Magnetism A force exerted by magnets. A magnet can attract certain material, and push or pull other magnets.

Matter Any material substance, solid, liquid or gas.

Observation Using your senses to notice something. Observations can be made during an experiment.

Philosophy The study of important questions about existence. Some theories can never be proved true or false.

Physicist A scientist involved in the study of forces and energy.

Radioactivity The process during which atoms break up. Radioactivity can produce harmful radiation.

Solar eclipse When the Moon passes between the Sun and the Earth, its shadow falls on the Earth and makes the Earth dark for a few minutes.

Species A particular type of plant or animal.

Technology Any machine or process that makes a certain task easier or quicker.

Theory An explanation that may be tested to find out whether it is correct.

INDEX *(Entries in **bold** refer to an illustration)*